GETTING STARTED
IN SIGNING

LIVING LANGUAGE®

Getting Started in Signing

Elaine Costello, Ph.D.

Illustrated by
**Lois A. Lehman
Linda C. Tom**

LIVING LANGUAGE,
A RANDOM HOUSE COMPANY
NEW YORK

Copyright © 2000 by Living Language, A Random House Company

All rights reserved. No part of this book may be reproduced or
transmitted in any form or by any means, electronic or mechanical,
including photocopying, recording, or by any information storage and
retrieval system, without permission in writing from the publisher.

Published by Living Language, A Random House Company,
New York, New York.
Living Language is a member of the Random House Information
Group.

Random House, Inc. New York, Toronto, London, Sydney, Auckland

www.livinglanguage.com

Living Language and colophon are registered trademarks of
Random House, Inc.

Printed in the United States of America

Design by Elaine Costello

Library of Congress Cataloging-in-Publication Data available
upon request.

ISBN 0-609-80653-X

10 9 8 7 6 5 4 3 2 1

First Edition

Table of Contents

Acknowledgments

The contribution of Deaf people in the preparation of this book cannot be overstated. The signs in this book are a snapshot in time of American Sign Language, the living and ever-changing language of the Deaf community. As a modest attempt at simplifying a vibrant, complex language, this book may fall short. But, it is hoped that by making American Sign Language more accessible for hearing people to study and learn, Deaf people will be rewarded for sharing their unique language.

I want to thank the two talented Deaf artists, Lois Lehman and Linda Tom, who drew the fine sign illustrations for the book with realistic precision. I also want to acknowledge the many Deaf informants who modeled the signs and helped identify the best signs to include.

Ken Visser, Systems Manager at Fontana Lithograph, Inc., in Cheverly Maryland, and Dennis Stevens, Webmaster and Graphic Artist for the Department of Defense at the Pentagon, generously provided technical assistance for the design and production of the book. I appreciate their time in helping me hone my fledgling production skills.

Without the support of the editors at Random House's Living Language, this book and the accompanying videotape would not have come to fruition. I am grateful to Christopher Warnasch and Christopher Medellín who helped ensure the quality and integrity of the work. Special thanks go to the rest of the Living Language team: Lisa Alpert, Elizabeth Bennett, Helen Tang, Elyse Tomasello, Zviezdana Verzich, Suzanne McGrew, Pat Ehresmann, and Linda Schmidt.

Introduction

Welcome!

You are about to learn a fascinating language that is unlike any other language in the world. Instead of a language of sounds like all spoken languages, American Sign Language is a visual language formed by organized hand gestures, movements, and facial expressions.

Who Uses American Sign Language?

American Sign Language (ASL) is the native language of about 400,000 people in the United States. Most of the native users are deaf, but some native users are the hearing children and other relatives of Deaf* people. A *native* language is the first language a person learns, and it is learned naturally through interaction with other users.

Approximately 600,000 hearing and Deaf people use ASL or some form of sign language on a daily basis. Relatives, neighbors and co-workers of Deaf people are among the hearing people who learn sign language. Some people are able to learn ASL as a second language and become proficient enough to use it as fluently as a native signers.

Deaf is spelled with a capital *D* when referring to members of the Deaf community.

Although ASL has its roots in French Sign Language, it is unique to North America. Most countries have their own sign language with their own signs and structure. No universal sign language exists. Do not misunderstand sign language as a word-for-word translation of English, either. It has its own word order and structure, often very different form spoken English.

Conceptual Signing

Signs are the phonological units of ASL. Signs cannot be paired one-to-one with English words; instead signs represent concepts. Usually English words are used to *gloss,* or represent, the meaning of a sign because ASL has no written form. When English glosses are written to represent signs, they appear in capital letters. Sometimes a "string" of signs is necessary to express a concept that requires only one English word to say. When more than one English word is used to "translate" a sign, the English words are hyphenated as in the following example:

undecided

NOT-YET   DECIDE

In contrast, sometimes a series of English words are needed to express a concept that ASL can express compactly in one sign.

six months

SIX-MONTHS

Getting Started in Sign

This book will introduce you to a basic sign vocabulary, sufficient to converse in sign language with Deaf people. The videotape that accompanies this book reviews many essential grammatical rules of the structure of ASL and shows you how these signs are used. This program will get you started in ASL, but in order to become proficient, make sure you take advantage of every opportunity to meet and mingle with Deaf people. Use every opportunity to try out your signs so that you learn to use them fluently.

The good news is that Deaf people will be able to communicate with you even if you use the signs you learn in this book in the sequence of English sentences. Deaf people know both ASL and English, and when they realize you are signing in an English word order, they will *code-switch* and accommodate your signing style.

If you are trying to sign a concept, but you don't know a sign, you can always spell out the English word using *fingerspelling*. Fingerspelling is the letter-by-letter spelling of English words using the hand-shapes of the American Manual Alphabet (see pages 23-24). Usually fingerspelling is used for words for which there is no sign, such as proper names and technical terms.

Let's learn some basic signs to get you started.

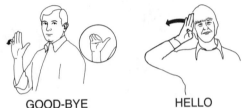

GOOD-BYE   HELLO

Now you are ready to greet Deaf people. Did you notice that these signs are natural gestures for their concepts? GOODBYE is simply a farewell wave and HELLO salutes a greeting. Many signs are easy to remember because they are natural gestures.

Let's learn two more basic concepts, YES and NO. The sign YES looks like the shape of a head nodding in the affirmative. The sign NO is a quick combination of the fingerspelled letters N and O.

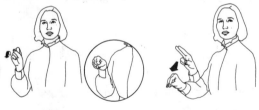

YES   NO

ASL is more than hand gestures; ASL uses facial expression and body movement as an integral part of the language. Be sure and nod your head when indicating an affirmative answer, and shake your head whenever you are giving a negative response.

Here are some signs you can use to be polite. First, PLEASE, which is like rubbing the chest with pleasure, and THANK YOU, which seems to bring words of gratitude from the mouth. And the hand seems to be rubbing out pain in your heart when you sign SORRY.

PLEASE   THANK-YOU   SORRY

Here are two signs that are not so easily remembered. Try to think of mnemonic hints that help you remember the signs: EXCUSE ME and YOU'RE WELCOME. Can you think of mnemonic clues for them?

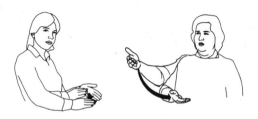

EXCUSE-ME   YOU'RE WELCOME

Doesn't EXCUSE ME look like you are brushing away an offense? And doesn't YOU'RE WELCOME look like you are welcoming the other person in close to you?

Signs Have Variations

ASL is a living language and, like all languages, it changes over time. As technology and concepts come into vogue, ASL users develop new signs that become part of the language. Historically, for ease and speed of formation, signs that used to be formed with two hands are now formed with one hand. Signs have also moved inward toward the center of the chest where they can be observed more easily.

ASL also accommodates regional variations. Signs are developed by communities of users as necessary for communication. As Deaf people travel and use their signs with other Deaf people, the variations become apparent. As you learn sign language, don't be dismayed to see more than one sign for the same concept. These variations are a product of a living, growing language.

Enjoy your experience in learning sign language, have fun with it, and don't forget to practice with native users, Deaf people. Good luck.

A Guide to Using This Book

The signs in this book are arranged in the order that they appear in the accompanying videotape. Each part in the book corresponds with a lesson in the videotape. The signs are best learned by viewing the video and then using this book with line drawings to help recall how the signs are made.

Many of the signs in the book may be conceptually translated with more than one English word. These alternate glosses are given with each illustration. All of the glosses are listed alphabetically in the index at the end of the book. The index is helpful to search for a particular sign.

Each entry in this book consists of a line drawing of the sign and a description of each of the four parts of the sign. Look at the four parts of the sign NOT.

NOT
Handshape: 10
Orientation: palm left
Location: under chin
Movement: forward
Note: Sign may be accompanied with a negative headshake.

Handshape. When a sign is fromed with only one hand, the handshape is given for the dominant hand (i.e., usually the right hand). When two hands are used, the handshape for the dominant hand is given first and separated by a colon from the handshape for the other hand. The notations RH for right hand and LH for left hand are used, presuming that the right hand is the dominant hand for the signer. Left-handed signers should reverse the directions in the sign as necessary. If the handshape of either hand changes during the formation of the sign, that change is noted here, too (e.g., A changes to S : open).

Most of the handshapes are taken from the American Manual Alphabet and from numbers. Some handshapes are unique or are modifications. Some of these handshapes are as follows:

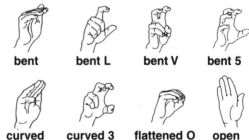

| bent | bent L | bent V | bent 5 |

| curved | curved 3 | flattened O | open |

Orientation. The direction that the palm faces when making a sign can make a difference in the meaning of the sign. The palm orientation is described as follows: right, left, up, down, in, forward. The palm orientation is given for the initial position when beginning to execute the sign. The position of the hands with one another is also described in this section.

Location. "Neutral space" is indicated for most of the signs. This refers to the space just in front of the lower chest where the hands most naturally can move and where the receiver's eye can most easily see the signs. About 90 percent of all signs are formed in this location. In this section, the initial location (e.g., thumb on chin) indicates where the sign begins prior to any movements.

Movement. The arrows on the drawings show the movement used in executing the sign. To further clarify the movement, the text describes the movement telling when the hands move in (e.g., downward in an arc). The ending position of the hands is described including the location and palm orientation.

Note. The "note" section is used for indication of non-manual cues, if necessary; for variations in sign formation that are permissible; and for other information that may help you use the sign appropriately.

Glossary

conceptual signing – choosing to use a sign based on the concept being expressed and not the equivalent English word

fingerspelling – the spelling out of each letter of an English word by using the American Manual Alphabet

gloss – an English word that represents the same concept as a sign; glosses are usually written with capital letters.

iconic – signs that look like an aspect of its referent

manual communication – a generic term used to refer to any communication formed on the hands

non-manual cue – a facial expression or other body language that contributes to the meaning of a sign

referent – the person or thing being discussed

sign – a meaningful gesture that represents a concept and can be described by its handshape, palm orientation, location, and movement

signer – the person using sign language

Part One

The Family Reunion

MOTHER, MAMA, MOM, MOMMY
Handshape: 5
Orientation: palm left
Location: thumb on chin
Movement: tap thumb twice on chin

FATHER, DAD, DADDY, PAPA
Handshape: 5
Orientation: palm left
Location: thumb on forehead
Movement: tap thumb twice on forehead

GRANDMOTHER
Handshape: 5
Orientation: palm left
Location: thumb on chin
Movement: hand moves
forward in double arc

GRANDFATHER
Handshape: 5
Orientation: palm left
Location: thumb on
forehead
Movement: hand moves
forward in double arc

COUSIN (female)
Handshape: C
Orientation: palm left
Location: near right side
of chin
Movement: twist wrist
back and forth
Note: Form the sign near
the right temple for a male.

AUNT
Handshape: A
Orientation: palm forward
Location: near right side of chin
Movement: shake hand

UNCLE
Handshape: U
Orientation: palm forward
Location: near the right temple
Movement: shake hand

NIECE
Handshape: N
Orientation: palm left
Location: near right side of chin
Movement: twist hand forward and back

NEPHEW
Handshape: N
Orientation: palm left
Location: near the right temple
Movement: twist hand forward and back

BOY
Handshape: flattened C
Orientation: palm left
Location: thumb side on right side of forehead
Movement: close fingers and thumb together with a double movement

GIRL
Handshape:10
Orientation: palm down
Location: thumb on right cheek
Movement: brush thumb toward chin with a double movement

BABY, INFANT
Handshape: open : open
Orientation: both palms up
Location: neutral space;
right arm resting on bent
left arm
Movement: swing arms
from side to side

DAUGHTER
Compound Sign:
GIRL + BABY

SON
Compound Sign:
BOY + BABY

SAME, ALIKE, AS, IDENTICAL, LIKE, SUCH
Handshape: 1 : 1
Orientation: both palms down, index fingers pointing forward
Location: apart in neutral space
Movement: bring sides of index fingers together

BROTHER
Compound Sign:
BOY + SAME

SISTER
Compound Sign:
GIRL + SAME

**POLITE, COURTEOUS,
COURTESY, GENTLE,
MANNERS, PRIM**
Handshape: 5
Orientation: palm left
Location: thumb on chest
Movement: tap thumb on
chest with a double movement

MAN, GENTLEMAN, MALE
Compound Sign: modified
form of BOY + POLITE

WOMAN, FEMALE, LADY
Compound Sign:
GIRL + POLITE

MARRY
Handshape: curved :
curved
Orientation: RH palm down
above LH; LH palm up
Location: neutral space
Movement: bring palms
together

HUSBAND
Compound Sign: modified
form of BOY + MARRY

WIFE
Compound Sign: modified
form of GIRL + MARRY

FAMILY
Handshape: F : F
Orientation: RH palm
left; LH palm right
Location: neutral space
Movement: move hands
away from each other in
outward arcs while turning
palms in, ending with little
fingers together

ME, I
Handshape: 1
Orientation: palm right,
index finger pointing in
Location: near chest
Movement: touch chest
with the extended index finger

HE, SHE, IT
Handshape: 1
Orientation: palm down,
index finger pointing
toward referent
Location: neutral space
Movement: jab index finger
toward referent

YOU (singular)
Handshape: 1
Orientation: palm down,
index finger pointing forward
Location: neutral space
Movement: jab index
finger forward toward
referent

THEY, THEM
Handshape: 1
Orientation: palm down,
index finger pointing
toward referents
Location: neutral space
Movement: swing index
finger in an arc toward
referents

US
Handshape: U
Orientation: palm right,
ending with palm left,
fingers pointing up
Location: right side of chest
Movement: swing hand
from the right side of the
chest in an arc to the left
side of the chest

YOU (plural)
Handshape: 1
Orientation: palm down,
index finger pointing forward
Location: neutral space
Movement: swing the
index finger from pointing
forward in an arc to the right
toward referents

MY
Handshape: open
Orientation: palm in
Location: near chest
Movement: bring palm in
against chest

HIS, HER, ITS
Handshape: open
Orientation: palm toward
referent
Location: neutral space
Movement: push hand
toward referent

YOUR (singular)
Handshape: open
Orientation: palm forward
Location: neutral space
Movement: push hand
forward toward referent

YOUR (plural)
Handshape: open
Orientation: palm forward
toward referent
Location: neutral space
Movement: move hand
in an arc to the right
toward referents

THEIRS
Handshape: open
Orientation: palm toward
referent
Location: neutral space
Movement: push hand in
an arc toward referents

OUR
Handshape: curved
Orientation: palm left
Location: thumb on right
side of chest
Movement: swing the
hand in an arc from the
right to the left side of the
chest, ending with palm
facing right and little finger on chest

MYSELF
Handshape: A
Orientation: palm left
Location: thumb near chest
Movement: tap the thumb
against the chest with a
double movement

HIMSELF, HERSELF, ITSELF
Handshape: A
Orientation: palm left
Location: neutral space
Movement: push thumb
toward referent

YOURSELF
Handshape: A
Orientation: palm left
Location: neutral space
Movement: push thumb
forward toward referent

THEMSELVES
Handshape: A
Orientation: palm left
Location: neutral space
Movement: push thumb
in an arc toward
referents

YOURSELVES
Handshape: A
Orientation: palm left
Location: neutral space
Movement: move
hand in an arc to the
right toward referents

OURSELVES
Handshape: A
Orientation: palm left
Location: right side of chest
Movement: move hand
in an arc from the right to
touch the left side of the
chest

PERSON MARKER
Handshape: open : open
Orientation: palms facing
each other
Location: in front of each
side of body
Movement: downward
along sides of the body

**TEACH, EDUCATE,
INDOCTRINATE, INSTRUCT**
Handshape: flattened O :
flattened O
Orientation: RH palm left;
LH palm right
Location: near each side
of the head
Movement: forward with a
short double movement

TEACHER
Compound Sign:
TEACH + person
marker

ACT, DRAMA, PERFORM,
PLAY, SHOW, THEATER
Handshape: A : A
Orientation: palms facing
each other
Location: each side of chest
Movement: downward with
alternating circular movements

ACTOR, ACTRESS,
PERFORMER
Compound Sign:
ACT + person
marker

CAMERA
Handshape: L : bent L
Orientation: palms
facing each other
Location: near each
side of the head
Movement: bend the right
index finger down

PHOTOGRAPHER
Compound
Sign:
CAMERA +
person marker

WRITE, EDIT, SCRIBBLE
Handshape: baby O : open
Orientation: RH palm down;
LH palm up
Location: neutral space
Movement: RH moves
with a wiggling movement
from heel to fingers of left
palm

WRITER, AUTHOR, EDITOR
Compound Sign: WRITE + person marker

SELL, MERCHANDISE, PEDDLE, RETAIL, SALE, VEND
Handshape: flattened O : flattened O
Orientation: both palms down
Location: neutral space
Movement: bend wrists up and down

SALESCLERK, MERCHANT, SALESPERSON, SELLER, VENDOR
Compound Sign: SELL + person marker

SERVE, SERVICE, WAIT ON
Handshape: open : open
Orientation: both palms up
Location: apart in front of each side of body
Movement: forward and back with an alternating movement

WAITER, WAITRESS, SERVER
Compound Sign:
SERVE +
person marker

ARMY
Handshape: A : A
Orientation: both palms in, right hand above left hand
Location: right side of chest
Movement: tap palm side of both hands against chest with a double movement

SOLDIER
Compound Sign:
ARMY + person
marker

HAIRCUT
Handshape: V
Orientation: palm down
Location: near right cheek
Movement: open and
close fingers while moving
back along side of head
Note: This sign can be
signed with two hands.

BARBER,
BEAUTICIAN,
HAIR STYLIST
Compound Sign:
HAIRCUT +
person marker

LAW
Handshape: L : open
Orientation: palms facing
each other, fingers
pointing forward
Location: neutral space
Movement: tap right
palm on left palm, first near
the fingers and then on
the heel

**LAWYER,
ATTORNEY
Compound Sign:**
LAW + person
marker

LEARN
Handshape: 5 changes
to flattened O : open
Orientation: RH fingers on
left palm; palms facing
Location: neutral space
Movement: RH hand moves
upward to right side of forehead
while changing to flattened O

STUDENT, PUPIL
Compound Sign:
LEARN +
person marker

American Manual Alphabet

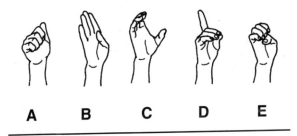

A   B   C   D   E

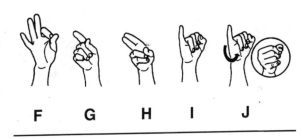

F   G   H   I   J

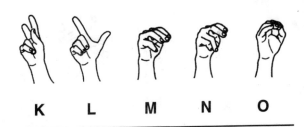

K   L   M   N   O

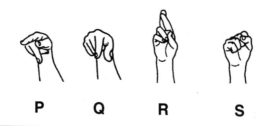

P   Q   R   S

T   U   V   W

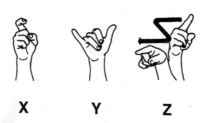

X   Y   Z

Part Two

Saturday at Home

BOX, PACKAGE, PRESENT, ROOM
Handshape: open : open
Orientation: RH palm left changing to palm in; LH palm right, changing to palm in
Location: neutral space
Movement: bend wrists, moving LH near body and RH somewhat forward

HOUSE
Handshape: open : open
Orientation: palms angled toward each other, fingertips touching
Location: neutral space
Movement: bring hands down and apart from each other a short distance, and then straight down

---

HOME
Handshape: flattened O
Orientation: palm down
Location: right side of chin
Movement: touch fingertips
first on the right side of the
chin and then on the right
cheek

WALL
Handshape: B : B
Orientation: both palms
forward, index fingers
touching each other and
fingers pointing up
Location: in front of face
Movement: bring hands
straight apart from each other

FLOOR
Handshape: B : B
Orientation: both palms
down, index fingers touching
each other and fingers
pointing forward
Location: in front of waist
Movement: bring hands
straight apart from each other

WINDOW
Handshape: B : B
Orientation: both palms
in, fingers pointing in
opposite directions,
RH above LH
Location: neutral space
Movement: bring right
little finger down on left index
finger with a double movement

DOOR
Handshape: B : B
Orientation: both palms
forward, fingers pointing up
Location: neutral space
Movement: swing RH to
the right, ending with
palm left

TABLE, DESK
Handshape: open : open
Orientation: both palms
down, bent right arm on
bent left arm
Location: neutral space
Movement: tap arms together
with small double movement

POLISH, RUB
Handshape: A : open
Orientation: both palms
down; RH on back of LH
Location: neutral space
Movement: rub right
knuckles across back of
LH with a repeated movement

CHAIR, SEAT
Handshape: H : H
Orientation: both palms
down, right fingers curved
across left fingers
Location: neutral space
Movement: tap right fingers
across left fingers
Note: Similar to SIT except
made with double movement

SIT
Handshape: H : H
Orientation: both palms
down, right fingers curved
across left fingers
Location: neutral space
Movement: place right
fingers across left fingers
Note: Similar to CHAIR
except made with single movement

EAT
Handshape: flattened O
Orientation: palm down,
fingers pointing in
Location: near lips
Movement: move fingertips
to the lips
Note: Similar to FOOD except
made with single movement

FOOD
Handshape: flattened O
Orientation: palm down,
fingers pointing in
Location: near lips
Movement: move fingertips
to the lips with a small
double movement
Note: Similar to EAT except
made with double movement

COUCH, PEW, SOFA
Compound Sign: SIT
+ LOAF (as follows)
Handshape: C : C
Orientation: both
palms down
Location: neutral
space
Movement: move both C hands
from in front of the body apart to each side

FURNITURE
Handshape: F : F
Orientation: palms apart and facing forward, fingers pointing up
Location: neutral space
Movement: shake both hands with a short side-to-side movement
Note: This sign may be made with one hand.

LAMP, LIGHT, SHINE
Handshape: flattened O changes to 5 : open
Orientation: RH palm down, bent elbow resting on left palm; LH palm up
Location: neutral space
Movement: move RH slightly downward while opening the fingers

LIGHT
Handshape: 8 changes to 5
Orientation: palm in
Location: in front of mouth
Movement: flick middle finger open

LIVING ROOM
Compound
Sign:
POLITE +
BOX

DINING ROOM
Compound
Sign: EAT +
BOX

BED
Handshape: open : open
Orientation: palms together,
LH on top of RH
Location: left cheek
Movement: lay cheek on
back of left hand

BEDROOM
Compound
Sign: BED +
BOX

BATH
Handshape: 10 : 10
Orientation: both palms in
Location: on each side of
chest
Movement: rub palm sides
of both hands up and down
on chest

BATHROOM
Compound
Sign: BATH +
BOX

REST ROOM
Handshape: R
Orientation: palm down
Location: neutral space
Movement: bounce down
with a double movement

COOK, BAKE, FLIP,
FRY, TURN OVER
Handshape: open : open
Orientation: RH palm
down across LH, palm up
Location: neutral space
Movement: flip RH over
and back on left palm

KITCHEN
Handshape: K : open
Orientation: RH palm
down across left palm;
LH palm up
Location: neutral space
Movement: flip RH over
ending with back of RH
on left palm

CLEAN
Handshape: open : open
Orientation: RH palm
down across left palm;
LH palm up
Location: neutral space
Movement: wipe right
palm across left palm
from heel to the fingers

FIND, DISCOVER, PICK UP
Handshape: 5 changes to F
Orientation: palm down
Location: in front of right
side of body
Movement: bring hand up
while closing thumb and
index finger

USE, UTILIZE
Handshape: U : S
Orientation: RH palm
forward, heel on back of
LH, fingers pointing up; LH
palm down
Location: neutral space
Movement: move RH in
small circle, hitting back of
LH each time it passes

SEE, PERCEIVE, SIGHT, VISUALIZE
Handshape: V
Orientation: palm in, fingers pointing at eyes
Location: in front of eyes
Movement: bring hand forward a short distance

LOOK AT
Handshape: V
Orientation: palm down, fingers pointing forward
Location: neutral
Movement: move hand forward a short distance

PLAY (*v.*)
Handshape: Y : Y
Orientation: palms facing each other
Location: neutral
Movement: twist wrists up and down with a repeated movement

WAIT
Handshape: 5 : 5
Orientation: both palms apart and up, fingers curved and pointing forward
Location: neutral space
Movement: wiggle fingers with a repeated movement

REST, RECESS, RELAX, RETIRE
Handshape: open : open
Orientation: both palms in, wrists crossed on the chest
Location: each side of chest
Movement: lay palms on chest near opposite shoulder

GET, ACQUIRE, OBTAIN, PROCURE, RECEIVE
Handshape: 5 changes to S : 5 changes to S
Orientation: palms facing opposite directions
Location: neutral space
Movement: bring hands toward chest, ending with little-finger side of right S handon thumb side of left S hand

SWEEP
Handshape: open : open
Orientation: RH palm in,
little-finger side on left palm;
LH palm up
Location: neutral space
Movement: brush right
little finger toward the heel
of left palm

FIX, MEND, REPAIR
Handshape: flattened O :
flattened O
Orientation: palms facing
each other, fingertips touching
Location: neutral space
Movement: move hands
up and down with a double
movement brushing fingertips
across each other

WASH, RUB, WIPE
Handshape: A : A
Orientation: palms facing
each other; RH on top of LH
Location: neutral space
Movement: rub right knuckles
across left knuckles with a
repeated movement

KEEP, MAINTAIN
Handshape: K : K
Orientation: palms facing
in opposite directions;
RH on top of LH
Location: neutral space
Movement: tap little-
finger side of RH on
thumb side of LH

ON
Handshape: open : open
Orientation: both palms
down; RH above LH
Location: neutral space
Movement: bring palm of
RH down across back of LH

OFF
Handshape: open : open
Orientation: both palms
down; RH across LH
Location: neutral space
Movement: raise RH a
short distance

OVER, ACROSS, AFTER, AFTERWARD, CROSS
Handshape: open : open
Orientation: RH palm left; LH palm down
Location: neutral space
Movement: slide little-finger side of RH across back of LH

UNDER
Handshape: 10 : open
Orientation: RH palm left; LH palm down, fingers pointing right
Location: neutral space
Movement: move RH from near chest, forward under left palm

IN FRONT OF, AHEAD, BEFORE
Handshape: 10 : 10
Orientation: palms facing each other
Location: neutral space
Movement: move RH in an arc to the front of the LH

BEHIND, BACKSIDE
Handshape: 10 : 10
Orientation: palms facing
in opposite directions;
RH in front of LH
Location: neutral space
Movement: move RH in
an arc toward the chest,
ending behind LH

TO
Handshape: 1 : 1
Orientation: RH palm down,
finger pointing forward; LH
palm in, finger pointing up
Location: neutral space
Movement: move right
index finger a short distance
forward to meet left index finger

FROM
Handshape: X : 1
Orientation: palms facing
in opposite directions; right
knuckle touching left index
finger
Location: neutral space
Movement: bring RH in
toward chest

IN, INTERNAL
Handshape: flattened O:
flattened O
Orientation: RH palm down;
LH palm in; RH above LH
Location: neutral space
Movement: move right
fingertips into thumb side
opening of LH

OUT, GET OUT, GO OUT
Handshape: 5 changes to
flattened O : C
Orientation: RH palm down;
LH palm right; right fingers
in thumb side opening of LH
Location: neutral space
Movement: bring right hand
upward closing fingers to
flattened O

WITH
Handshape: A : A
Orientation: palms apart
facing each other
Location: neutral space
Movement: bring hands
together

WITHOUT
Handshape: A changes to
5: A changes to 5
Orientation: palms together
facing each other
Location: neutral space
Movement: bring hands
apart while opening fingers

HAT
Handshape: open
Orientation: palm down
Location: above head
Movement: pat top of head
with a double movement

DOG
Handshape: open
Orientation: palm left
Location: near right thigh
Movement: pat right thigh
with a double movement

CRACKER
Handshape: A
Orientation: palm up
Location: near elbow of
bent left arm
Movement: tap palm side
of RH on left elbow with
a repeated movement

BRIDGE
Handshape: V
Orientation: palm left,
fingers pointing up
Location: right fingers near
wrist of bent left arm
Movement: move the right
fingers from the wrist to
the elbow of the left arm

WHAT
Handshape: 1 : open
Orientation: RH palm left,
index finger in left palm;
LH palm up
Location: neutral space
Movement: bring right
index finger down across
left palm

WHO
Handshape: 1
Orientation: palm in, index
finger pointing toward lips
Location: in front of mouth
Movement: move finger in
small circle in front of lips

WHICH
Handshape: 10 : 10
Orientation: palms
apart facing each
other
Location:
neutral space
Movement: move hands
up and down with an
alternating movement

WHY
Handshape: bent
changes to Y
Orientation: palm in
Location: right side of
forehead
Movement: hand moves
forward while changing to
Y hand

WHEN
Handshape: 1 : 1
Orientation: palms facing, RH above LH and fingers pointing toward each other
Location: neutral space
Movement: move right index finger in circular movement around and landing on left index finger

HOW MUCH
Handshape: curved : curved
Orientation: palms apart facing each other
Location: neutral space
Movement: move hands apart a short distance

WHERE
Handshape: 1
Orientation: palm forward
Location: neutral space
Movement: shake finger from side to side with a double movement

HOW
Handshape: curved : curved
Orientation: palms facing in opposite directions, knuckles touching
Location: fingers on chest
Movement: twist fingers up, ending with palms up

HOW MANY
Handshape: S changes to 5
Orientation: palm up
Location: neutral space
Movement: flick fingers open quickly
Note: This sign may be made with two hands.

QUESTION
Handshape: 1 changes to X changes back to 1
Orientation: palm forward, finger pointing forward
Location: in front of right shoulder
Movement: bend and then straighten index finger forming a question mark as the hand moves downward

Part Three

The Doctor's Appointment

DEAF

Handshape: 1
Orientation: palm in
Location: on upper cheek near ear
Movement: touch the cheek first near the ear and then near the right side of the mouth

---

BLIND

Handshape: bent V
Orientation: palm in
Location: in front of eyes
Movement: jab fingertips in toward eyes

HEART
Handshape: 5
Orientation: palm in
Location: near left side
of chest
Movement: tap the bent
middle finger on the chest
with a double movement

HEART ATTACK
Compound sign: HEART
+ ATTACK (as follows)
Handshape: S : open
Orientation: both
palms in; RH nearer
chest than LH
Location: neutral space
Movement: hit left palm
with knuckles of RH

PNEUMONIA
Handshape: P : P
Orientation: both palms in
Location: each side of chest
Movement: rub middle
finger of both hands up
and down on chest

COLD (illness)
Handshape: A
Orientation: palm in
Location: nose
Movement: with the thumb
and index finger holding the
nose, pull forward off the
nose with a short double
movement

FAINT
Handshape: 1 changes
to 5 : 5
Orientation: palms down
Location: RH forehead; LH
in front of left side of body
Movement: RH down to in
front of right side of chest while
changing to 5 hand

PREGNANT
Handshape: 5 : 5
Orientation: palms in,
fingers pointing toward
each other
Location: in front
of stomach
Movement: bring
hands together, inter-
locking the fingers

SICK
Handshape: 5 : 5
Orientation: both palms in
Location: RH near forehead;
LH near stomach
Movement: touch RH bent
middle finger to forehead
and LH bent middle finger
to stomach
Note: This sign may be made with RH only.

DIZZY, WOOZY
Handshape: curved
Orientation: palm left
Location: near right side
of head
Movement: move the hand
in a repeated circular movement
Note: This sign may be made
with two curved hands on
each side of the head

UPSET
Handshape: open
Orientation: palm in
Location: on stomach
Movement: flip the
hand forward, ending
with palm up

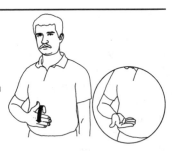

VOMIT
Handshape: 5 : 5
Orientation: palms facing
each other; RH nearer
the mouth than the LH
Location: RH near mouth;
LH somewhat forward
Movement: move both
hands forward in large arcs

COUGH
Handshape: S
Orientation: palm down
Location: on chest
Movement: hit thumb side of
RH against the chest with a
double movement

**BREATHE, BREATH, EXPEL,
INHALE, PANT, RESPIRATION**
Handshape: 5 : 5
Orientation: both palms in;
fingers pointing toward
each other; RH above LH
Location: in front of chest
Movement: move hands
forward and back with a
double movement

TEMPERATURE
Handshape: 1 : 1
Orientation: RH palm in,
finger pointing left; LH
palm right, finger pointing up
Location: neutral space
Movement: slide right
index finger up and down
on left index finger

PAIN, ACHE, INJURY
Handshape: 1 : 1
Orientation: RH palm down;
LH palm up; fingers pointing
toward each other
Location: neutral space
Movement: twist wrists in
opposite directions

EYE
Handshape: 1
Orientation: palm in
Location: in front of eye
Movement: point finger
toward eye with a short
double movement

NOSE
Handshape: 1
Orientation: palm down
Location: near nose
Movement: touch finger
to nose

TEETH
Handshape: X
Orientation: palm in
Location: in front of mouth,
lips open
Movement: move finger
from right to left across teeth

TONGUE
Handshape: 1
Orientation: palm in
Location: in front of mouth,
tongue slightly extended
Movement: touch finger
to the tongue

STOMACH
Handshape: bent
Orientation: palm up;
fingers pointing in
Location: near stomach
Movement: tap fingers on
stomach with a double
movement

FOOT
Handshape: 5 : open
Orientation: both palms
down; RH over LH
Location: neutral space
Movement: move right
bent middle finger up and
down the back of LH with
a repeated movement

KNEE
Handshape: bent
Orientation: palm left
Location: near right knee
Movement: tap fingertips
on knee with a double
movement

ELBOW
Handshape: 1
Orientation: palm up
Location: left elbow
Movement: touch the elbow
with the extended index
finger

BODY
Handshape: open : open
Orientation: both palm in
fingers pointing toward
each other
Location: each side
of chest
Movement: fingers touch
each side of the chest and
then each side of the waist

HEAD
Handshape: bent
Orientation: palm down;
fingers pointing left
Location: right side of
forehead
Movement: fingers touch
right side of forehead and
then right side of chin

FACE, LOOKS
Handshape: 1
Orientation: palm in;
finger pointing in
Location: near face
Movement: with the index
finger, draw a circle around
face

MOUTH
Handshape: 1
Orientation: palm in;
finger pointing in
Location: near mouth
Movement: with the index
finger, draw a circle around
mouth

EAR
Handshape: A
Orientation: palm left
Location: near earlobe
Movement: wiggle the
earlobe with the index
finger and thumb

NECK
Handshape: bent
Orientation: palm down;
fingers pointing left
Location: near right side
of neck
Movement: tap fingertips
to neck with a double
movement

BACK
Handshape: open
Orientation: palm down;
fingers pointing back
Location: over right
shoulder
Movement: pat fingers
behind right shoulder with
a repeated movement

ARM
Handshape: curved
Orientation: palm down;
RH curved over left wrist
Location: left wrist
Movement: slide right palm
up extended left arm from
the wrist to above the elbow

HANDS
Handshape: B : B
Orientation: palms angled down and toward each other; little finger of RH across thumb of LH
Location: neutral space
Movement: bring RH down under LH to exchange positions; repeat with LH

MEDICINE
Handshape: 5 : open
Orientation: RH palm down above LH; LH palm up
Location: neutral space
Movement: with bent middle finger of RH in left palm, rock RH from side to side

PILL, TAKE A PILL
Handshape: A
Orientation: palm in
Location: in front of mouth
Movement: beginning with index finger tucked under thumb, flick index finger toward mouth with a double movement

**INJECTION, HYPODERMIC,
SHOT, VACCINE**
Handshape: L
Orientation: palm in;
finger pointing left
Location: upper left arm
Movement: with right index
finger against upper left arm,
bend right thumb down

SURGERY, OPERATE
Handshape: A : open
Orientation: RH palm down;
LH palm up; RH on top of LH
Location: neutral space
Movement: move right
thumb from fingers to heel
of left palm

DOCTOR
Handshape: D
Orientation: palm left, on
wrist of LH, palm up
Location: neutral space
Movement: tap heel of
RH on left wrist with a
double movement

NURSE
Handshape: N
Orientation: palm down,
on wrist of LH, palm up
Location: neutral space
Movement: tap fingertips
of RH on left wrist with
a double movement

**MEDICAL, DOCTOR,
PHYSICIAN**
Handshape: M
Orientation: palm down,
on wrist of LH, palm up
Location: neutral space
Movement: tap fingertips
of RH on left wrist with
a double movement

HOSPITAL
Handshape: H
Orientation: RH
palm back, fingers
pointing left
Location: upper
left arm
Movement: move right
fingers down and then
from back to front on left arm

AMBULANCE
Handshape: flattened O
changes to 5 changes
back to flattened O
Orientation: palm
forward
Location: in front of
right shoulder
Movement: twist hand back and
forward while opening and closing the fingers

**HEALTHY, BOLD, CURE,
HEAL, STRENGTH,
STRONG, WELL**
Handshape: 5 changes
to S : 5 changes to S
Orientation: both palms
back, fingers pointing up
Location: each side of chest
Movement: bring hands
forward while closing the fingers

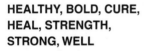

HELP, ASSIST
Handshape: A : open
Orientation: RH palm left,
little finger on left palm;
LH palm up
Location: neutral space
Movement: push RH up
with LH

HEALTH, HUMAN, HYGIENE
Handshape: H : H
Orientation: both palms in, fingers apart and pointing toward each other
Location: each side of chest
Movement: move both hands down to touch each side of waist

HURT, ACHE, HARM, WOUND
Handshape: 1 : 1
Orientation: both palms in; fingers pointing toward each other
Location: neutral space
Movement: jab fingers toward each other with a short double movement

EARACHE
Locational Sign: HURT signed near the ear.

STOMACHACHE
Locational Sign: HURT
signed near the stomach.

HEADACHE
Locational Sign: HURT
signed near the forehead.

BANDAGE
Handshape: H : open
Orientation: both
palms down; RH
above LH
Location: neutral
space
Movement: slide right
fingers across back of LH

LONELY
Handshape: 1
rientation: palm left
Location: mouth
Movement: slide index
finger slowly downward
in front of mouth

ROCK
Handshape: S : S
Orientation: both palms
down; RH on top of LH
Location: neutral space
Movement: tap palm side
of RH on back of LH with
a double movement

SURGERY, OPERATE
Locational Sign: SURGERY
signed on the stomach, the
location of surgery.

Part Four

The Picnic

ROSE
Handshape: R
Orientation: palm in
Location: nose
Movement: touch fingers
first to right side and then
left side of nose

WAY, CORRIDOR, HALL,
PATH, ROAD, STREET
Handshape: open : open
Orientation: palms apart
facing each other; fingers
pointing forward
Location: neutral space
Movement: move hands
forward

WAY
Handshape: W : W
Orientation: palms apart facing each other; fingers pointing forward
Location: neutral space
Movement: move hands forward

STREET
Handshape: S : S
Orientation: palms facing each other
Location: neutral space
Movement: move hands forward

ROAD
Handshape: R : R
Orientation: palms facing each other; fingers pointing forward
Location: neutral space
Movement: move hands forward

PATH, PARALLEL
Handshape: P : P
Orientation: palms facing
each other; index fingers
pointing forward
Location: neutral space
Movement: move hands
forward

CLASS, CATEGORY,
GROUP
Handshape: C : C
Location: neutral space
Movement: move
hands away from each
other in outward arcs while
turning palms in, ending with little fingers together

GROUP
Handshape: G : G
Orientation: palms
facing each other
Location: neutral space
Movement: move
hands away from each
other in outard arcs
while turning palms in and
ending with little fingers together

ORGANIZATION
Handshape: O : O
Orientation: palms facing
forward; fingertips touching
Location: neutral space
Movement: move hands
away from each other in
outward arcs while turning
palms in and ending with
little fingers together

SOCIETY
Handshape: S : S
Orientation: palms facing
forward; thumbs touching
Location: neutral space
Movement: move hands
away from each other in
outward arcs while turning
palms in and ending with
little fingers together

TEAM
Handshape: T : T
Orientation: palms facing
forward; thumbs touching
Location: neutral space
Movement: move hands
away from each other in
outward arcs while turning
palms in and ending with
little fingers together

HOTDOG

Handshape: G changes to Baby O : G changes to Baby O
Orientation: palms facing each other; fingers touching
Location: neutral space
Movement: move hands outward to each side while pinching index fingers and thumbs together with a repeated movement

HAMBURGER

Handshape: curved : curved
Orientation: palms facing each other; RH on top of LH
Location: neutral space
Movement: flip hands over, ending with LH on top of RH

SANDWICH

Handshape: open : open
Orientation: palms facing each other; RH on top of LH; fingers pointing to mouth
Location: mouth
Movement: move fingers toward mouth with a short double movement

SAUSAGE
Handshape: C changes to
S: C changes to S
Orientation: palms facing
forward; thumbs touching
each other
Location: neutral space
Movement: move hands
outward to each side while
opening and closing the hands

BACON
Handshape: H with thumb
extended : H with thumb
extended
Orientation: palms facing
each other; fingers touching
Location: neutral space
Movement: move hands
outward to each side while bending
the fingers with a repeated movement

MEAT
Handshape: F : open
Orientation: RH palm
down; LH palm in
Location: neutral space
Movement: while grasping
the LH near the base of the
index finger with the right
index finger and thumb,
shake the hands slightly

BREAD

Handshape: bent : open
Orientation: RH palm in, fingers touching back of LH; LH palm in, fingers pointing right
Location: neutral space
Movement: move right fingertips down back of LH with a repeated movement

FRENCH FRIES
Handshape: F
Orientation: palm down
Location: neutral space
Movement: dip fingers down first in front of body and again slightly to the right

POTATO
Handshape: bent V : open
Orientation: both palms down, RH over LH
Location: neutral space
Movement: tap right fingertips on back of LH with a double movement

VEGETABLE
Handshape: V
Orientation: palm left,
fingers pointing up
Location: right cheek
Movement: beginning with
index finger touching right
cheek, twist hand to touch
middle finger to chin,
ending with palm facing back

SALAD
Handshape: curved : curved
Orientation: both palms
up, hands apart, fingers
pointing toward each other
Location: near each side
of the body
Movement: move hands
toward each other in a
double circular movement

PANCAKE
Handshape: open : open
Orientation: RH, palm up
on LH, palm up
Location: neutral space
Movement: flip RH over,
ending with palm down

SYRUP
Handshape: 1
Orientation: palm down
Location: upper lip
Movement: wipe finger
from under nose to right
cheek

TOAST
Handshape: V : open
Orientation: palms facing
each other; right fingertips
in left palm
Location: neutral space
Movement: swing RH
around to touch fingertips
to back of LH

BUTTER
Handshape: H with thumb
extended : open
Orientation: palms facing
each other; right fingertips
on left palm
Location: neutral space
Movement: wipe right fingers
across left palm with a repeated movement,
closing right fingers back into palm each time

JELLY
Handshape: J : open
Orientation: RH palm in,
fingertip on left palm; LH
palm up
Location: neutral space
Movement: strike right little
finger against left palm as
it moves upward with a
double movement

EGG
Handshape: H : H
Orientation: both palms in;
right fingers across left
fingers
Location: neutral space
Movement: move hands
downward and away from
each other with a double
movement

DRINK[1] (*n.*)
Handshape: C
Orientation: palm left
Location: near mouth
Movement: keeping the
thumb near the chin, tip hand
upward toward the face with
a short double movement

Note: Similar to the verb form of this sign
except made with a quick double movement

DRINK[2] (*v.*)
Handshape: C
Orientation: palm left
Location: near mouth
Movement: keeping the
thumb near the chin, tip
hand upward toward the face
Note: Similar to the noun
form of the sign except made
with a longer, slower movement.

WATER
Handshape: W
Orientation: palm left
Location: mouth
Movement: tap index
finger against mouth with
a double movement

MILK
Handshape: C changes
to S
Orientation: palm left
Location: neutral space
Movement: squeeze
fingers open and closed
with a double movement

COFFEE
Handshape: S : S
Orientation: palms facing
in opposite directions;
RH on top of LH
Location: neutral space
Movement: rub little-finger
side of RH on index-finger
side of LH with a circular
movement

TEA
Handshape: F : O
Orientation: RH palm
down, fingers inserted in
thumb side of LH; LH
palm right
Location: neutral space
Movement: move right
fingertips in small circle
in hole formed by LH

SODA
Handshape: 5 changes
to open : O
Orientation: RH palm down,
bent middle finger in thumb
side of LH; LH palm right
Location: neutral space
Movement: pull right bent
middle finger from hole formed
by LH; then slap right palm on thumb side of LH

DESSERT
Handshape: D : D
Orientation: palms facing each other; index fingers pointing up
Location: neutral space
Movement: tap the fingertips of both hands together with a repeated movement

COOKIE, BISCUIT
Handshape: C : open
Orientation: RH palm down, fingers touching left palm; LH palm up
Location: neutral space
Movement: touch right fingertips on left palm; twist RH and touch fingertips to the left palm again

CAKE
Handshape: C : open
Orientation: RH palm down, fingers touching left palm; LH palm up
Location: neutral space
Movement: slide fingertips of RH from heel to fingers of left palm and then perpendicular of left palm

PIE
Handshape: open : open
Orientation: RH palm
left, fingers touching
left palm; LH palm up
Location: neutral
space
Movement: slide
fingertips of RH across
left palm at several angles

ICE CREAM
Handshape: S
Orientation: palm left
Location: in front of mouth
Movement: move hand
back to mouth in a
double circular movement

POPCORN
Handshape: S changes
to 1 : S changes to 1
Orientation: both
palms in
Location: neutral space
Movement: alternately,
with a repeated movement,
move each hand upward
while flicking up each index finger**Handshape:** K

PEPPER
Handshape: P
Orientation: palm down
Location: neutral space
Movement: shake hand
downward with a short
repeated movement

SALT
Handshape: V : V
Orientation: both palms down
Location: neutral space, right
fingers across left fingers
Movement: with a quick
alternatingly motion, tap
right fingers on back of left
hand.

WEATHER
Handshape: W : W
Orientation: palms facing
each other
Location: neutral space
Movement: keeping
thumbs and little fingers
of both hands touching the
other hand, twist hands in opposite
directions with a double movement

COLD, CHILLY, FRIGID, SHIVER, WINTER
Handshape: S : S
Orientation: palms apart facing each other
Location: neutral space
Movement: holding arms stiff, shake both hands with a small repeated movement

HOT, HEAT
Handshape: curved
Orientation: palm in
Location: in front of mouth
Movement: twist wrist, throwing hand forward and slightly downward

WARM
Handshape: E changes to C
Orientation: palm in
Location: in front of mouth
Movement: move hand from mouth forward in a small arc while opening fingers

COOL, AIR, PLEASANT, FRESH

Handshape: open changes to bent : open changes to bent
Orientation: palms back
Location: near each side of head
Movement: bend fingers up and down with a double movement

SUN, GRACE, SUNLIGHT, SUNSHINE

Handshape: flattened O changes to 5
Orientation: palm forward
Location: above right side of head
Movement: twist palm back and flick fingers open

CLOUD

Handshape: C : C
Orientation: palms facing each other
Location: above left side of head
Movement: turn palms in, ending with little fingers near each other; repeat above right side of head

RAIN
Handshape: curved : curved
Orientation: both palms
down .
Location: in front of each
side of the head
Movement: bring hands
downward with a double
movement

SNOW
Handshape: 5 : 5
Orientation: both
palms down
Location: thumbs
touching each shoulder
Movement: bring hands
slowly forward and down
while wiggling the fingers

SUMMER
Handshape: 1 changes to X
Orientation: palm down
Location: left side of
forehead
Movement: pull the index
finger to the right across
the forehead while bending
the finger

FALL, AUTUMN
Handshape: B
Orientation: palm down
Location: near elbow of
bent left arm
Movement: brush right
index finger downward with
a double movement toward
left elbow

TREE
Handshape: 5
Orientation: palm back;
fingers pointing up
Location: near right side
of head
Movement: with the right
elbow on the back of the LH,
twist the right palm forward
and back with a repeated movement

SPRING
Handshape: flattened O
changes to 5 : C
Orientation: RH palm up,
fingers pointing up near
left palm; LH palm right
Location: neutral space
Movement: move RH upward
through the LH with a double
movement, opening the fingers each time

GROW, SPROUT
Handshape: flattened O
changes to 5 : C
Orientation: RH palm up,
fingers pointing up near
left palm; LH palm right
Location: neutral space
Movement: move RH
upward through the LH
while opening the fingers

WIND, STORM
Handshape: 5 : 5
Orientation: palms apart
facing each other; fingers
pointing forward
Location: neutral space
Movement: wave the hands
with a back and forth movement
Note: Move the hands more
quickly for a stronger wind or storm.

STORM, CHAOS,
DISORDER, MESSY, RIOT
Handshape: curved : curved
Orientation: palms apart
facing each other; RH
above LH
Location: neutral space
Movement: twist hands
with a deliberate movement
reversing positions

TORNADO
Handshape: 1 : 1
Orientation: both palms in;
RH above LH; fingers
pointing toward each other
Location: neutral space
Movement: move right
finger upward while circling
above left finger

HURRICANE
Handshape: 5 : 5
Orientation: both palms in;
RH above LH; fingers
pointing toward each other
Location: neutral space
Movement: move RH
upward while making
circles around LH

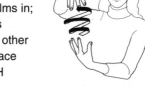

FLOOD
Compound Sign:
WATER + water
rising (as follows)
Handshape: 5 : 5
Orientation: both
palms down; fingers
pointing forward
Location: neutral space
Movement: raise hands slowly in front of body

RAINBOW
Handshape: 4
Orientation: palm in;
fingers pointing left
Location: in front of left
side of chest
Movement: bring hand
upward in an arc in front
of the chest, ending with
fingers pointing up

MORNING
Handshape: open
Orientation: palm back;
fingers pointing up, LH in
the bend of the right arm
Location: in front of right
side of body
Movement: with LH in the
bend of the right arm, raise
RH to in front of right shoulder

NOON
Handshape: open
Orientation: palm forward
Location: in front of the
right side of the body
Movement: rest the elbow
of the bent right arm on the
back of the LH held across
the body

AFTERNOON, MATINEE
Handshape: open
Orientation: palm down;
right forearm on back of LH
Location: neutral space
Movement: with the right
forearm resting on the back
of the LH held across the
chest, move RH down with
a short double movement

NIGHT, TONIGHT
Handshape: bent
Orientation: palm down;
heel of RH on back of LH
Location: neutral space
Movement: tap the heel of
RH with a double movement
on back of LH held across
the chest

**MIDNIGHT, MIDDLE OF
THE NIGHT**
Handshape: B
Orientation: palm left,
fingers pointing down
Location: near right hip
Movement: with left fingers
in crook of extended right
arm, swing RH to the left

GOOD, WELL
Handshape: open : open
Orientation: RH palm in,
fingers pointing up;
LH palm up
Location: RH near mouth;
LH neutral space
Movement: bring RH down
to land back of RH in palm
of LH

Part Five

Our Vacation

BREAKFAST[1]
Compound Sign:
EAT + MORNING

BREAKFAST[2]
Handshape: B
Orientation: palm left
Location: mouth
Movement: tap index
finger to chin with a
double movement

DINNER[1]
Compound Sign:
EAT + NIGHT

DINNER[2]
Handshape: D
Orientation: palm in
Location: mouth
Movement: tap fingertips
to chin with a double movment

LUNCH[1]
Compound Sign:
EAT + NOON

LUNCH[2]
Handshape: L
Orientation: palm left
Location: mouth
Movement: tap thumb
to chin with a double
movement

FLY
Handshape: thumb,
index finger, and little
finger extended
Orientation: palm down
Location: in front of
right shoulder
Movement: move hand
forward and upward
with a long movement

AIRPLANE, JET, PLANE
Handshape: thumb,
index finger, and little
finger extended
Orientation: palm down
Location: in front of
right shoulder
Movement: move hand
forward and upward with
a short double movement

CAR, AUTOMOBILE
Handshape: S : S
Orientation: palms apart
facing each other;
LH higher than RH
Location: in front of each
side of the chest
Movement: move hands
up and down with short
repeated alternating movements

DRIVE
Handshape: S : S
Orientation: palms apart
facing each other;
LH higher than RH
Location: in front
each side of the chest
Movement: move hands
up and down with large
repeated alternating movements

GAS, FUEL, GASOLINE
Handshape: 10 : S
Orientation: RH palm
forward, thumb down; LH
palm right; RH above LH
Location: neutral space
Movement: dip right
thumb into thumb-side
opening of LH with a short
double movement

FILL-UP
Handshape: 10 : S
Orientation: RH palm forward, thumb left; LH palm right; RH above LH
Location: neutral space
Movement: move right wrist to the left in an arc to dip the right thumb into thumb-side opening of LH

VACATION
Handshape: 5 : 5
Orientation: palms apart facing each other
Location: thumbs near each armpit
Movement: keeping thumbs touching near each armpit, wiggle the fingers of both hands

CAMPING, TENT
Handshape: index and little fingers extended : index and little fingers extended
Orientation: palms angled toward each other; extended fingers touching
Location: neutral space
Movement: move hands downward and apart with a double movement

HOTEL
Handshape: H : 1
Orientation: RH palm in, fingers pointing left; LH palm in, finger pointing up
Location: neutral space
Movement: touch the right extended fingers to the back of the left extended finger

CITY, COMMUNITY
Handshape: open : open
Orientation: RH palm angled back, LH palm angled forward, fingertips pointing up and touching
Location: in front of chest
Movement: twist wrists and touch fingertips again, ending with RH palm angled forward and LH palm angled back

---

COUNTRY
Handshape: open
Orientation: palm in, fingers left, on elbow of bent left arm
Location: left elbow
Movement: rub right palm in a circle on left forearm with a repeated movement

MOUNTAIN
Compound Sign:
ROCK + HILL
(as follows)
Handshape:
open : open

Orientation: palms angled
down, fingers angled up
Location: neutral space
Movement: upward and forward

VALLEY
Handshape: B : B
Orientation: palms down,
fingers pointing forward
Location: in front of
each shoulder
Movement: move hands
downward toward each other,
ending with index fingers touching
in front of body

RIVER
Compound Sign:
WATER + FLOW
(as follows)
Handshape: 5 : 5
Orientation: both
palms apart and
down, fingers pointing forward
Location: neutral space
Movement: forward with a wavy movement

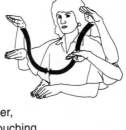

FOREST, WOODS
Handshape: 5
Orientation: palm back, fingers pointing up
Location: near right side of face

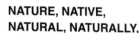

Movement: with the right elbow on the back of the LH, twist the right palm forward and back while moving the arms to the right each time

---

NATURE, NATIVE, NATURAL, NATURALLY, OF COURSE
Handshape: N : open
Orientation: palms down; RH above LH
Location: neutral space
Movement: move RH in small circle over back of LH and then straight down to touch right fingertips on back of LH

TRAIN, RAILROAD
Handshape: H : H
Orientation: both palms down; right finger across left fingers
Location: neutral space
Movement: rub right fingers back and forth on back of left fingers

SHIP, CRUISE
Handshape: 3 : open
Orientation: RH palm left
on left palm; LH palm up
Location: neutral space
Movement: with little-
finger side of RH on
left palm, move both hands
forward

BICYCLE, BIKE, PEDAL
Handshape: S : S
Orientation: both palms
apart and down, RH
lower than LH
Location: neutral space
Movement: move both
hands in large alternating forward
circles

TRAFFIC
Handshape: 5 : 5
Orientation: palms
facing each other;
fingers pointing up
Location: neutral
space
Movement: move hands forward and
back with a repeated movement, brushing
palms as the hands move past each other

PARK

Handshape: 3 : open
Orientation: RH palm left
above left palm; LH palm up
Location: neutral space
Movement: tap little-finger
side of RH in left palm
with a repeated movement

CANOE, OAR

Handshape: S : S
Orientation: both palms
in, RH higher than LH
Location: in front of right
side of chest
Movement: swing both
hands downward to the left
side of the body with a double
movement

HORSE

Handshape: H with
thumb extended
Orientation: palm forward
Location: right side of head
Movement: bend fingers
up and down with a double
movement
Note: This sign may be made
with two hands.

RIDE (a horse)
Handshape: 3 : open
Orientation: RH palm in,
fingers pointing down
straddling left index finger;
LH palm right
Location: neutral space
Movement: with right fingers
straddling index-finger side of LH,
move both hands forward in a double arc

THEATER
Handshape: A : A
Orientation: palms apart
facing each other
Location: on each side
of the chest
Movement: move the
thumbs downward and forward
with an alternating circular movement
on each side of the chest

MOVIE, FILM, SHOW
Handshape: 5 : open
Orientation: RH palm
forward, fingers pointing
up; LH palm in, fingers
pointing right
Location: neutral space
Movement: with the heel of the right
hand on the left palm, twist the right
hand from side to side with a repeated movement

ART, DRAWING, ILLUSTRATION, SKETCH
Handshape: I : open
Orientation: RH palm in, little finger pointing up and touching left fingers; LH palm right, fingers pointing up
Location: neutral space
Movement: RH down with a wiggly movement from the LH fingers to the heel

MUSEUM
Handshape: M : M
Orientation: both palms forward, fingers together
Location: neutral space
Movement: move hands apart to in front of each shoulder and then straight down

COME
Handshape: 1 : 1
Orientation: both palms up
Location: neutral space
Movement: bring fingers in to each side of the chest

GO TO
Handshape: 1 : 1
Orientation: both
palms forward, RH
closer to chest than LH
Location: neutral space
Movement: bend both
wrists down, ending with
index fingers pointing
forward

**LEAVE, DEPART,
WITHDRAW**
Handshape: 5
to flattened O :
5 to flattened O
Orientation:
both palms down
Location: in front of chest
Movement: back to chest while
closing the fingers and thumbs

ARRIVE, REACH
Handshape: bent : curved
Orientation: RH palm left,
fingers up; LH palm up
Location: in front of right
shoulder
Movement: bring the back
of the RH down to land in left palm

VISIT
Handshape: V : V
Orientation: both palms apart and back, fingers pointing up
Location: in front of each side of the chest
Movement: move hands forward in repeated alternating circles

TRAVEL, ADVENTURE, FIELD TRIP
Handshape: bent V
Orientation: palm down
Location: neutral space
Movement: upward and forward in a large arc

RIDE (in a car, truck, etc.)
Handshape: bent V : C
Orientation: RH palm down, fingers hooked over left thumb; LH palm right
Location: neutral space
Movement: move hands forward

PIANO, ORGAN
Handshape: 5 : 5
Orientation: both palms apart and down, fingers pointing forward
Location: neutral space
Movement: move hands from side to side in front of the body while wiggling the fingers

GUITAR
Handshape: F : curved 5
Orientation: RH palm in; LH palm right
Location: RH in front of right side of body; LH in front of left shoulder
Movement: twist RH down with a double movement

MUSIC, MELODY, SING, SONG
Handshape: open : open
Orientation: RH palm left over left palm, fingers forward; LH palm up
Location: neutral space
Movement: swing little-finger side of RH over left palm with a double movement

MAGAZINE, BROCHURE, PAMPHLET
Handshape: A : open
Orientation: RH palm left, thumb and index finger holding little-finger side of LH; LH palm up
Location: neutral space
Movement: slide RH from the heel to the fingertips of LH with a double movement

NEWSPAPER, PRESS, PUBLICATION
Handshape: G changes to baby O : open
Orientation: RH palm down above left palm; LH palm up
Location: neutral space
Movement: pull RH down toward heel of LH, closing right thumb to index finger

TELEVISION, TV
Quickly fingerspell T-V

TICKET
Handshape: bent V : open
Orientation: RH palm down
near little-finger side of
LH; LH palm in, fingers
pointing up
Location: neutral space
Movement: move the bent right
fingers on each side of the little-
finger side of LH with a double movement

STAGE
Handshape: S : open
Orientation: RH palm
forward; LH palm down,
fingers pointing right
Location: neutral space
Movement: slide heel of RH
from the wrist to the fingers
of LH

EXERCISE, WORK OUT
Handshape: S : S
Orientation: palms
facing each other
Location: near each
shoulder
Movement: move hands
outward with a double movement

JOG
Handshape: S : S
Orientation: palms apart and facing each other, one hand higher than the other
Location: in front of each side of body
Movement: move both hands in repeated outward circles

PLAY CARDS, CARDS
Handshape: A : A
Orientation: palms facing each other, index fingers touching
Location: neutral space
Movement: move RH forward with a small repeated movement

READ
Handshape: V : open
Orientation: RH palm down, fingers touching left palm; LH palm right, fingers pointing up
Location: neutral space
Movement: move right fingers from the left fingertips to the heel

BOOK

Handshape: open : open
Orientation: palms facing and together, fingers angled forward
Location: neutral space
Movement: bring hands apart at the top while keeping the little fingers together

DANCE

Handshape: V : open
Orientation: RH palm in, fingers pointing down above left palm; LH palm up
Location: neutral space
Movement: swing right fingers over left palm with a double movement

CAT

Handshape: F
Orientation: palm facing in
Location: near right side of the mouth
Movement: pull hand outward toward each cheek with a short repeated movement
Note: This sign may be formed with two hands.

FRAME
Handshape: G : G
Orientation: palms facing
each other, fingers touching
Location: neutral space
Movement: move hands
apart to in front of each
shoulder, then straight
down, then back together in
front of the lower chest

**MANY, A LOT,
NUMEROUS**
Handshape: S changes
to 5 : S changes to 5
Orientation: both
palms up
Location: in front of
each side of the chest
Movement: flick the fingers open
quickly with a double movement

ALL, ENTIRE, WHOLE
Handshape: open : open
Orientation: RH palm
forward, hand above
LH; LH palm in
Location: RH in front
of upper chest; LH
neutral space
Movement: move RH in large circle
around LH, ending with back of RH in left palm

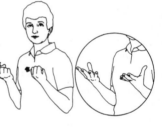

HORDE, CROWD, MASS
Handshape: curved 5 : curved 5
Orientation: both palms down
Location: in front of upper chest
Movement: move both hands forward
Note: Follow movement of the hands with the eyes.

FROG
Handshape: S changes to H
Orientation: palm down, fingers pointing left
Location: chin
Movement: flick index and middle fingers outward with a double movement

SQUIRREL
Handshape: bent V : bent V
Orientation: palms facing each other, heels and fingertips touching
Location: neutral space
Movement: keeping heels together tap the fingertips together with a double movement

COW
Handshape: Y
Orientation: palm forward
Location: thumb on
side of forehead
Movement: keeping
thumb on the forehead,
twist hand forward
Note: This sign may be
made with hands.

THERE, POINT
Handshape: 1
Orientation: palm down,
finger pointing forward
Location: neutral space
Movement: push finger
forward

Part Six

A Holiday Get-Together

CHRISTMAS
Handshape: C
Orientation: palm forward
Location: in front of left shoulder
Movement: move hand in an arc to in front of right shoulder

HANUKKAH or **CHANUKAH**
Handshape: B changes to 4 : B changes to 4
Orientation: palms forward, fingers pointing up
Location: near each other in front of the chest
Movement: bring hands outward to the sides of the chest while opening the fingers

Days of the Week

Monday   **Tuesday**   **Wednesday**

Thursday   **Friday**

Saturday   **Sunday**

THANKSGIVING
Handshape: G
Orientation: palm left
Location: nose
Movement: bring hand
down in an arc to
the chest

**HALLOWEEN, MASK,
MASQUERADE**
Handshape: curved :
curved
Orientation: palms in,
fingers pointing up, little
fingers touching
Location: in front of eyes
Movement: bring hands apart
around head while turning the forward

VALENTINE
Handshape: 5 : 5
Orientation: both palms
in; bent middle fingers
touching chest near
each other
Location: left side of chest
Movement: move bent
middle fingers in a heart
shape downward on chest

DAY
Handshape: 1
Orientation: palm left,
finger pointing up
Location: near right
side of the head
Movement: with the right
elbow on the back of the LH

held across the chest, bring right index
finger downward toward the left elbow

THINK
Handshape: 1
Orientation: palm down,
index finger pointing left
Location: right side of
forehead
Movement: tap the index
finger against the forehead

MIND, BRAIN, SENSE
Handshape: X
Orientation: palm back,
index finger pointing in
Location: right side of
forehead
Movement: tap the index
finger against the forehead

DREAM, DAYDREAM
Handshape: 1 changes to X
Orientation: palm down,
index finger pointing left
Location: right side of
forehead
Movement: bring the index
finger outward to the right,
bending the finger up and down as
the hand moves

WONDER, CONSIDER,
CONTEMPLATE,
MEDITATE, PONDER,
REFLECT, THINK ABOUT
Handshape: 1
Orientation: palm down,
index finger pointing in
Location: right side forehead
Movement: move index finger
in a small repeated circle

KNOW
Handshape: bent
Orientation: palm down,
fingers pointing left
Location: right side of
forehead
Movement: tap fingertips
on right side of the forehead

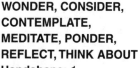

**INVENT, CREATE,
MAKE UP, ORIGINATE**
Handshape: 4
Orientation: palm left,
fingers pointing up
Location: right side of
forehead
Movement: slide index-finger
side of hands upward in an outward arc

MEMORIZE
Handshape: 1 changes
to S
Orientation: palm down,
finger pointing left
Location: right side of
forehead
Movement: bring hand forward
while closing the fingers

REMEMBER
Handshape: 10 : 10
Orientation: RH palm
left; LH palm down
Location: RH on
forehead; LH neutral space
Movement: bring right
thumb down to touch left thumb

AGREE, IN ACCORD, COMPATIBLE, COMPROMISE, SUIT
Compound Sign: THINK + SAME

JUDGE, COURT, JUSTICE, TRIAL
Handshape: F : F
Orientation: palms facing each other, RH higher than LH
Location: in front of each side of the chest
Movement: move hands up and down with a repeated alternating movement

DECIDE, DETERMINE, MAKE UP YOUR MIND,
Handshape: 1 changes to D : D
Orientation: RH palm left; LH palm right
Location: RH forehead; LH neutral space
Movement: move right hand down to near the left hand; then move both hands down a short distance

BELIEVE
Compound Sign:
THINK + MARRY

UNDERSTAND,
COMPREHEND,
PERCEIVE
Handshape: S changes
to 1
Orientation: palm left
Location: right side of
forehead
Movement: flick index finger
upward with a double movement

FORGET
Handshape: open
changes to 10
Orientation: palm in,
fingers pointing left
Location: forehead
Movement: wipe fingers
across forehead to the right
while changing to 10 hand

GUESS, ASSUME, ESTIMATE

Handshape: curved changes to S
Orientation: palm left
Location: right side of forehead
Movement: downward to the left while changing to S hand

TIME

Handshape: X
Orientation: palm down
Location: neutral space
Movement: tap index finger on back of LH held across the chest

WATCH, TIMEPIECE, WRISTWATCH

Handshape: F
Orientation: palm down
Location: neutral space
Movement: place palm side of RH on back of left wrist held across the chest

CLOCK
Compound Sign: TIME
+ shape of clock face
(as follows)
Handshape: curved
L : curved L
Orientation: palms apart
facing each other
Location: in front of each
side of head

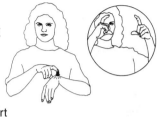

HOUR, ONE HOUR
Handshape: 1 : open
Orientation: palms
together facing each
other, fingers pointing up
Location: neutral space
Movement: move palm side
of RH in a circle on left palm

**MINUTE, MOMENT,
MOMENTARILY,
ONE MINUTE**
Handshape: 1 : open
Orientation: palms
together facing each
other, fingers pointing up
Location: neutral space
Movement: pivot palm side of
RH a quarter turn forward on left palm

SECOND, ONE SECOND
Handshape: 1 : open
Orientation: palms
together facing each
other, fingers pointing up
Location: neutral space
Movement: pivot palm side
of RH a short distance
forward on left palm

NUMBER
Handshape: flattened
O : flattened O
Orientation: LH
palm angled
forward; RH palm
facing in; fingers touching
Location: neutral space
Movement: move hands apart while twisting wrists
in opposite directions and touch fingertips again

HUNDRED
Handshape: C
Orientation: palm left
Location: neutral space
Movement: move right
a short distance

Numbers

1   **2**   **3**   **4**

5   **6**   **7**

8   **9**   **10**

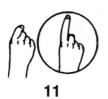

11

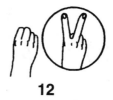

12

13

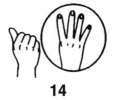

14

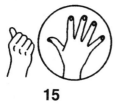

15

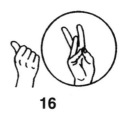

16

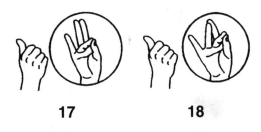

17   **18**

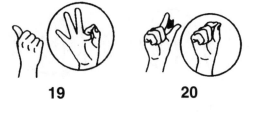

19   **20**

THOUSAND
Handshape: bent : open
Orientation: RH palm
down, fingers pointing
left; LH palm right
Location: neutral space
Movement: hit right
fingertips against left palm

MILLION
Handshape: bent : open
Orientation: RH palm
down, fingers pointing
left; LH palm right
Location: neutral space
Movement: hit right fingertips against left palm, first near
the heel and then near the fingers

WEEK, ONE WEEK
Handshape: 1 : open
Orientation: palms
together; right finger
pointing up; left fingers
pointing right
Location: neutral space
Movement: slide right
palm from the heel to
the fingers of the left palm

FOUR WEEKS
Handshape: 4 : open
Orientation: RH palm
down on left palm; LH palm up
Location: neutral space
Movement: slide heel of RH
from heel to fingers of
left palm

LAST WEEK
Handshape: 1 : open
Orientation: both palms
up, back of RH on left palm
Location: neutral space
Movement: slide back of RH
across left palm from the
heel off the fingers and up
toward right shoulder, ending with
right index finger pointing up

NEXT WEEK
Handshape: 1 : open
Orientation: palms facing
each other, RH on left palm
Location: neutral space
Movement: slide RH
across left palm and then
upward and forward in
an arc

WEEKLY
Handshape: 1 : open
Orientation: palms facing, RH above left palm; right finger pointing up; left fingers pointing right
Location: neutral space
Movement: move right finger

from the heel to the fingers of the left palm with a double circular movement

MONTH, ONE MONTH
Handshape: 1 : 1
Orientation: RH palm in, finger pointing left touching left finger; LH palm right, finger pointing up
Location: neutral space
Movement: slide right finger down the left finger

TWO MONTHS
Handshape: 2 : 1
Orientation: RH palm in, fingers pointing left touching left finger; LH palm right, finger pointing up
Location: neutral space
Movement: slide right finger down the left finger

MONTHLY
Handshape: 1 : 1
Orientation: RH palm in,
finger pointing left touching
left finger; LH palm right,
finger pointing up
Location: neutral space
Movement: slide right finger
down the left finger with a
double circular movement

YEAR
Handshape: S : S
Orientation: palms facing
each other; RH above LH
Location: neutral space
Movement: move RH in
a forward circle around LH,
ending with little-finger side
of RH on index-finger side of LH

NEXT YEAR
Handshape: S changes
to 1 : S
Orientation: palms facing
in opposite directions;
RH on top of LH
Location: neutral space
Movement: move RH
forward in an arc while
flicking index finger forward

LAST YEAR
Handshape: 1 changes
to X : S
Orientation: RH palm in,
finger pointing up, back
of RH on back of LH;
LH palm down
Location: neutral space
Movement: bend right index finger
up and down with a repeated movement

**ANNUALLY, EVERY YEAR,
PER ANNUM**
Handshape: S changes
to 1 : S
Orientation: palms facing
in opposite directions;
RH on top of LH
Location: neutral space
Movement: move RH forward while flicking index
finger forward with a double movement

EVERY MORNING
Handshape: open : open
Orientation: RH palm up,
fingers forward; LH, palm
in, fingers pointing right
in crook of right arm
Location: in front of left
side of body
Movement: swing RH from left
to right in front of body

EVERY NOON
Handshape: open : open
Orientation: RH palm left, fingers pointing up, bent elbow on back of LH; LH palm down, fingers pointing right
Location: in front of body
Movement: move arms to the right in front of body

EVERY AFTERNOON
Handshape: open : open
Orientation: RH palm down, fingers pointing forward, right forearm on back of LH; LH palm down, fingers pointing right
Location: in front of body
Movement: move arms to the right in front of the body

EVERY NIGHT
Handshape: open : open
Orientation: RH palm down, fingers pointing forward, heel on back of left wrist; LH palm down, fingers pointing right
Location: in front of the body
Movement: move arms to the right in front of the body

Part Seven

The Big Game

BASKETBALL
Handshape: 5 : 5
Orientation: palms apart
and facing each other,
fingers pointing forward
Location: in front of each
side of the chest
Movement: twist the
wrists upward with a double
movement

GOLF
Handshape: A : A
Orientation: RH palm
left; LH palm in
Location: RH down by
right hip; LH across
body near right hip
Movement: swing RH
up toward the left

BILLIARDS, POOL
Handshape: A : F
Orientation: RH palm
back, fingers down, elbow
extended back; LH palm
right, arm extended forward
Location: RH near right side of
chest; LH forward of right side of body
Movement: move RH forward
a short distance

SLED, SLEDDING
Handshape: bent V : open
Orientation: RH palm up
on back of LH; LH palm
down, fingers pointing right
Location: neutral space
Movement: push RH
forward off back of LH

HOCKEY
Handshape: X : open
Orientation: both palms up
Location: neutral space
Movement: move RH
upward in a circular
movement, brushing
right index finger on left
palm each time

FOOTBALL
Handshape: 5 : 5
Orientation: both palms facing down, fingers pointing toward each other
Location: neutral space
Movement: bring hands together with a double movement, interlocking fingers each time

SWIM, SWIMMING
Handshape: open : open
Orientation: both palms down, right fingers across left fingers
Location: neutral space
Movement: bring hands apart to the sides with a double movement

BOX, BOXING, FIGHT
Handshape: S : S
Orientation: both palms apart and down
Location: neutral space
Movement: move hands in a repeated circular movement toward each other

WRESTLE, WRESTLING
Handshape: 5 : 5
Orientation: palms facing
each other, fingers
interlocked
Location: neutral space
Movement: bend wrists
downward with a double
movement

VOLLEYBALL
Handshape: open : open
Orientation: both palms
forward, fingers pointing up
Location: near each side
of the head
Movement: push hands
upward and forward with
a double movement

BASEBALL, SOFTBALL
Handshape: S : S
Orientation: palms facing
in opposite directions;
little-finger side of RH on
index-finger side of LH
Location: in front of
right shoulder
Movement: move hands
downward across the body

ICE SKATING, SKATE
Handshape: X : X
Orientation: both palms up, fingers pointing forward, Rh forward of LH
Location: neutral space
Movement: move hands forward and back with a repeated and alternating swinging movement

HUNTING, HUNT
Handshape: L : L
Orientation: palms facing in opposite directions, fingers pointing forward, LH forward of RH
Location: in front of chest
Movement: move hands downward with a short double movement

TENNIS
Handshape: A
Orientation: palm left
Location: near left shoulder
Movement: swing hand downward to the right; repeat from near right shoulder

ROLLER SKATING, SKATE
Handshape: bent V : bent V
Orientation: both palms up, fingers pointing forward,
Location: neutral space

Movement: move hands forward and back with a repeated and alternating swinging movement

SOCCER
Handshape: B : B
Orientation: RH palm left, fingers pointing down; LH palm in, fingers pointing right
Location: RH near right side of body; LH neutral space
Movement: swing RH upward with a double movement, hitting the little-finger side of the left hand each time

BOWLING, BOWL
Handshape: curved 3
Orientation: palm forward, fingers pointing down
Location: near right hip
Movement: swing hand forward and upward

SKIING, SKI
Handshape: X : X
Orientation: both palms up; RH closer to chest than LH
Location: neutral space
Movement: move hands forward

RUN, RUNNING
Handshape: L : L
Orientation: palms facing in opposite directions, LH forward of RH
Location: neutral space
Movement: with right index finger hooked on left thumb, move hands forward

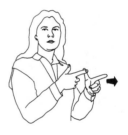

THROW, PITCH
Handshape: curved 3
Orientation: palm forward
Location: in front of right shoulder
Movement: forward and downward while turning palm down

CATCH[1] (a ball)
Handshape: 5 : 5
Orientation: palms facing
each other, fingers
pointing forward
Location: neutral
space
Movement: back
toward body while
constricting fingers

CATCH[2] (a robber)
Handshape: C : 1
Orientation: RH palm left;
LH palm right, finger
pointing up
Location: neutral space
Movement: move RH
to the left to grasp
extended left index finger

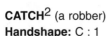

CATCH[3] (catch up)
Handshape: A : A
Orientation: palms facing
in opposite directions,
LH forward of RH
Location: neutral space
Movement: move right
thumb to heel of LH

WIN

Handshape: 5 changes to S : 5 changes to S
Orientation: RH palm left; LH palm left
Location: RH in front of right shoulder; LH neutral space
Movement: swing RH downward to the left across thumb side of LH while changing both hands to S hands, ending with right palm above LH

LOSE[1] (a game)

Handshape: V : open
Orientation: RH palm forward, fingers pointing up; LH palm up
Location: RH in front of right shoulder; LH neutral space
Movement: hit right palm on left palm

LOSE[2] (can't find)

Handshape: flattened O changes to 5 : flattened O changes to 5
Orientation: both palms up, fingers touching
Location: neutral space
Movement: drop both hands while opening fingers downward

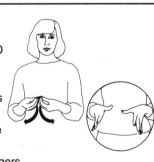

WALK
Handshape: 3 : 3
Orientation: both
palms down
Location: neutral
space

Movement: move hands forward
and back with an alternating
movement

STAND
Handshape: V : open
Orientation: RH palm in,
fingers pointing down on
left palm; LH palm up
Location: neutral space

JUMP
Handshape: V : open
Orientation: RH palm
in, fingers pointing
down on left palm;
LH palm up
Location: neutral space

Movement: move RH
up and down touching fingers
to left palm each time

FALL
Handshape: V : open
Orientation: RH palm
in, fingers pointing
down on left palm;
LH palm up
Location: neutral space
Movement: flip RH over,
ending with back of RH on left palm

**PUT, INSTALL, PLACE,
SET**
Handshape: flattened O :
flattened O
Orientation: both palms
down near each other
Location: neutral space
Movement: move hands
forward in a small arc

CARRY
Handshape: curved : curved
Orientation: both palms
up near each other
Location: in front of right
side of chest
Movement: move hands
in a series of arcs to the
left in front of body

HOLD, GRIP
Handshape: S
Orientation: palm up
Location: in front of right side of body
Movement: circular movement to the right

MAKE, CREATE, FORM, MANUFACTURE, PRODUCE
Handshape: S : S
Orientation: palms facing in opposite directions, right little finger on left index finger
Location: neutral space
Movement: twist hands in opposite directions, touching hands together again

BRING, DELIVER, TRANSPORT
Handshape: curved : curved
Orientation: both palms up near each other
Location: in front of right side of chest
Movement: move hands in a large arc to the left in front of body

**WORK, EMPLOYMENT,
LABOR, OCCUPATION, TASK**
Handshape: S : S
Orientation: RH palm
forward above LH;
LH palm down
Location: neutral space
Movement: tap heel of
RH on back of LH with a
double movement

WORKAHOLIC
Handshape: S : S
Orientation: both palms
down, RH on back of LH
Location: neutral space
Movement: move RH in
a repeated circular
movement striking back of
LH each time

STOP, CEASE, HALT, QUIT
Handshape: open : open
Orientation: RH palm left,
fingers pointing forward;
LH palm up
Location: neutral space
Movement: bring little-
finger side of RH across
left palm

**FINISH, ALREADY,
COMPLETE, DONE,
OVER**
Handshape: 5 : 5
Orientation: palms up
Location: neutral space
Movement: flip hands over,
ending with palms down
Note: This sign may be made with one hand.

**START, BEGINNING,
ORIGIN, SOURCE**
Handshape: 1 : open
Orientation: RH palm
down, finger pointing left
between index and middle
finger of LH; LH palm right
Location: neutral space
Movement: twist right index
finger, ending with right palm up

QUIT
Handshape: H : O
Orientation: RH palm in,
fingers inserted in opening
of LH; LH palm down
Location: neutral space
Movement: bring right
fingers upward, ending in front
of right shoulder,fingers pointing up

CELEBRATE, FESTIVAL, GALA, REJOICE
Handshape: X : X
Orientation: palms facing each other
Location: in front of each shoulder
Movement: move hands in repeated circles

WOW, WHEW
Handshape: 5
Orientation: palm in, fingers pointing left
Location: neutral space
Movement: shake hand up and down with a repeated movement

TRUE, ACTUAL, CERTAIN
Handshape: 1
Orientation: palm left, finger pointing up
Location: mouth
Movement: forward in an arc

RIGHT[1] (direction)
Handshape: R
Orientation: palm forward
Location: right side of
body
Movement: to the right
a short distance

RIGHT[2] (correct),
ACCURATE, CORRECT
Handshape: 1 : 1
Orientation: palms
facing in opposite
directions, RH above LH
Location: neutral space
Movement: hit right little
finger on index finger of LH

RIGHT[3] (privilege),
ALL RIGHT, PRIVILEGE
Handshape: open : open
Orientation: RH palm
left, fingers on left
palm; LH palm up
Location: neutral
space
Movement: slide right
little finger across left palm

CALL[1] (telephone),
PHONE (v.)
Handshape: Y
Orientation: palm left
Location: near right side
of face
Movement: bring palm
side of RH to right cheek,
little finger near mouth and
thumb near ear

CALL[2] (yell), **HOLLER,
YELL**
Handshape: C
Orientation: palm left
Location: around right
side of mouth

CALL[3] (name)
Handshape: H : H
Orientation: palms
angled in opposite
directions, right middle
finger across left index finger
Location: neutral space
Movement: move hands
forward in an arc

FIRE[1] (flames)
Handshape: 5 : 5
Orientation: both palms
in, hands apart, fingers
pointing up
Location: in front of waist
Movement: move hands
upward while wiggling the fingers
Note: This sign may be formed
with an alternating circular movement.

FIRE[2], TERMINATE
Handshape: open : B
Orientation: RH palm up;
LH palm in, fingers
pointing right
Location: neutral space
Movement: swing back of
RH across index-finger side of LH

FIRE[3], SHOOT
Handshape: L : L
Orientation: hands apart,
palms facing each other,
index fingers pointing forward
Location: in front of chest
Movement: bend index
fingers up and down with a
double movement

Part Eight

Shopping at
the Mall

BE[1], AM, IS, ARE
Handshape: 1
Orientation: palm left,
finger pointing up
Location: mouth
Movement: forward

BE[2]
Handshape: B
Orientation: palm left,
fingers pointing up
Location: mouth
Movement: forward

AM
Handshape: A
Orientation: palm left
Location: mouth
Movement: forward

IS
Handshape: I
Orientation: palm left
Location: mouth
Movement: forward

ARE
Handshape: R
Orientation: palm left
Location: mouth
Movement: forward

WAS
Handshape: W changes
to S
Orientation: palm left
Location: near right side
of face
Movement: back while
closing fingers to S hand

WERE
Handshape: W changes
to R
Orientation: palm left
Location: mouth
Movement: back while
changing to R hand

WILL
Handshape: W
Orientation: palm left
Location: mouth
Movement: forward

Colors

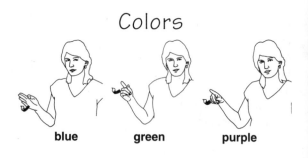

blue   **green**   **purple**

white   **red**

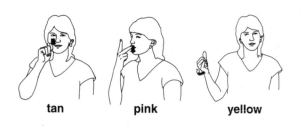

tan   **pink**   **yellow**

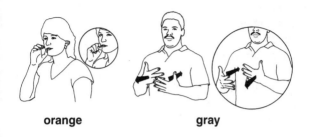

orange   **gray**

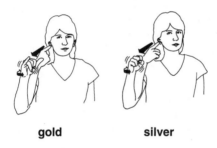

gold   **silver**

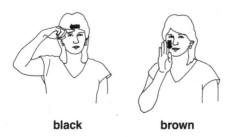

black   **brown**

COAT, JACKET
Handshape: A : A
Orientation: palms down, hands apart
Location: each side of chest
Movement: move thumbs down on chest toward each other to the waist

DRESS (*n.*), **CLOTHES**
Handshape: 5 : 5
Orientation: palms down, hands apart
Location: each side of chest
Movement: brush thumbs down on chest with a double movement
Note: The verb form of this sign is formed with one long movement down on the chest.

SKIRT
Handshape: 5: 5
Orientation: palms in, fingers pointing down
Location: each side of waist
Movement: move hands downward and outward with a double movement

BLOUSE

Handshape: open : open
Orientation: palms down, fingers apart and pointing toward each other
Location: each side of chest
Movement: bring hands down in outward arcs while turning the palms up, ending with both palms facing up

SLACKS, JEANS, PANTS, TROUSERS

Handshape: 5 : 5
Orientation: palms in, fingers pointing down
Location: each hip
Movement: pull fingers up toward the waist with a double movement

SHOES

Handshape: S : S
Orientation: both palms down, hands apart
Location: neutral space
Movement: tap index fingers together with a double movement

SOCKS
Handshape: 1 : 1
Orientation: both palms down, fingers pointing forward
Location: neutral space
Movement: move hands forward and back with an alternating movement, brushing sides of index fingers against each other

SHOP, SHOPPING
Handshape: flattened O : open
Orientation: both palms up; RH above LH
Location: neutral space
Movement: move RH forward with a double movement, brushing back of right fingers on left palm

BUY, PURCHASE
Handshape: flattened O : open
Orientation: both palms up, back of RH in left palm
Location: neutral space
Movement: move RH forward in an arc

MONEY, FUND
Handshape: flattened O : open
Orientation: both palm up, RH above left palm
Location: neutral space
Movement: tap back of RH on left palm with a double movement

SPEND
Handshape: S changes to curved : S changes to curved
Orientation: both palms up, fingers angled forward
Location: near each side of the body
Movement: move hands forward while slowly opening fingers

PAY
Handshape: 1 : open
Orientation: RH palm down, finger pointing down; LH palm up
Location: neutral space
Movement: move right index finger from heel to fingers of left palm

PRICE, COST, VALUE, WORTH
Handshape: F : F
Orientation: palms facing each other, fingers touching
Location: neutral space
Movement: tap fingertips together with a double movement

COST, CHARGE, FARE, FEE, FINE, PRICE, TAX
Handshape: X : open
Orientation: RH palm in, index finger knuckle on left palm; LH palm right, fingers pointing forward
Location: neutral space
Movement: bring right knuckle down on left palm

CHARGE, CREDIT CARD
Handshape: S : open
Orientation: RH palm left, little finger on left palm; LH palm up
Location: neutral space
Movement: RH hand rubs back and forth on left palm

DOLLAR
Handshape: flattened O :
open
Orientation: both palms
in, right fingers
holding left fingers
Location: neutral space
Movement: pull RH to
the right with a double
movement

COIN
Handshape: F : open
Orientation: RH palm left;
LH palm up
Location: neutral space
Movement: place right
curved fingers several
places on left palm

PENNY, CENT
Handshape: 1
Orientation: palm down
Location: right side of
forehead
Movement: forward with
a double movement

NICKEL, FIVE CENTS
Handshape: 5
Orientation: palm down,
bent middle finger
touching forehead
Location: right side of
forehead
Movement: forward with a
double movement

DIME, TEN CENTS
Handshape: 1 changes
to 10
Orientation: palm down
Location: right side of
forehead
Movement: forward while
changing to 10 hand, then
shake 10 hand

QUARTER,
TWENTY-FIVE CENTS
Handshape: 1 changes to 5
Orientation: palm down
Location: right side of
forehead
Movement: forward while
changing to 5 hand, then wiggle
bent middle finger of 5 hand

BROKE, PENNILESS
Handshape: bent
Orientation: palm down, fingers pointing back
Location: near right side of neck
Movement: hit little finger against neck
Note: Bend the neck to the left as if forced down from the impact.

LEND, LOAN
Handshape: V : V
Orientation: palms facing in opposite directions, right little finger across left index finger
Location: neutral space
Movement: forward and down a short distance

BORROW, LEND ME
Handshape: V : V
Orientation: palms facing in opposite directions, right little finger across left index finger
Location: neutral space
Movement: back toward the chest while turning the fingers up

TALL, HEIGHT
Handshape: bent
Orientation: palm down,
fingers pointing left
Location: near right
shoulder
Movement: raise hand
upward

SHORT (height),
LITTLE, SMALL
Handshape: bent
Orientation: palm down,
fingers pointing left
Location: near right side
of the body
Movement: move hand
downward with a short
double movement

FAT, CHUBBY
Handshape: curved :
curved
Orientation: palms facing
each other
Location: near each cheek
Movement: outward a short distance
Note: Puff out cheeks while forming the sign.

THIN, GAUNT, LEAN, SLIM, SKINNY
Handshape: G
Orientation: palm in
Location: in front of the mouth
Movement: down a short distance
Note: Suck in cheeks while forming the sign.

LONG, LENGTH
Handshape: 1
Orientation: palm in, finger pointing left touching wrist of extended left arm
Location: in front of the body
Movement: move right finger up the length of left arm from the wrist to the shoulder

SHORT (time)**, SOON, TEMPORARY**
Handshape: H : H
Orientation: palms angled toward each other
Location: neutral space; right middle finger across left index finger
Movement: rub right fingers back and forth with a short repeated movement on left fingers

BIG, ENLARGE, GROW BIG

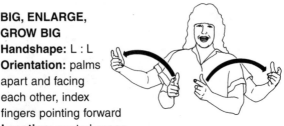

Handshape: L : L
Orientation: palms apart and facing each other, index fingers pointing forward
Location: neutral space
Movement: bring hands apart in large arcs

SMALL, LITTLE

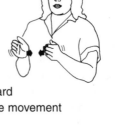

Handshape: open : open
Orientation: palms apart and facing each other, fingers pointing forward
Location: neutral space
Movement: move hands toward each other with a short double movement

---

WIDE

Handshape: open : open
Orientation: palms apart and facing each other, fingers pointing forward
Location: neutral space
Movement: move hands apart to in front of the sides of the body while turning the palms forward

---

NARROW
Handshape: open : open
Orientation: palms apart and facing each other, fingers pointing forward
Location: neutral space
Movement: move hands toward each other

THICK
Handshape: C : open
Orientation: RH palm forward, thumb on back of LH; LH palm down
Location: neutral space
Movement: slide right thumb from the left wrist to the fingers

THIN, SHORT
Handshape: G : open
Orientation: RH palm forward, thumb on back of LH; LH palm down
Location: neutral space
Movement: slide right thumb from the left wrist to the fingers

UGLY
Handshape: X
Orientation: palm left
Location: in front of
left cheek
Movement: move hand
to the right while
constricting the finger

**PRETTY, BEAUTIFUL,
LOVELY**
Handshape: 5 changes
to flattened O
Orientation: palm in
Location: in front of face
Movement: move hand
in a circle in front of face,
closing fingers to thumb in front of chin

HEAVY
Handshape: curved : curved
Orientation: both palms
apart and up
Location: in front of
each side of body
Movement: bring hands
down a short distance

LIGHT (weight)
Handshape: 5 : 5
Orientation: palms
down, fingers pointing forward
Location: in front of
each side of the body
Movement: with both middle
fingers bent, bring both hands
upward to in front of each side
of the chest while turning the palms up

OLD, ANTIQUE, QUAINT
Handshape: C changes
to S
Orientation: palm left
Location: in front of chin
Movement: bring hand
downward while closing
the fingers

NEW
Handshape: curved : curved
Orientation: both palms
up, RH above LH, fingers
pointing toward each other
Location: neutral space
Movement: slide back of
RH from the fingers to the heel
of the left palm

WET, DAMP, DEW, HUMID, MOIST
Handshape: 5 changes
to flattened O : 5 changes
to flattened O
Orientation: both palms
in, fingers pointing up
Location: RH chin; LH in front of chest
Movement: move hands down
while closing fingers to thumbs

DRY, BORING
Handshape: X
Orientation: palm down
Location: left side of chin
Movement: drag index
finger from left to right
across chin

POOR, PAUPER, POVERTY
Handshape: curved 5
changes to flattened O
Orientation: palm up,
fingers pointing up
Location: left bent elbow
Movement: pull RH down with
a double movement, closing
fingers to thumb each time

RICH, WEALTH
Handshape: S changes
to curved 5 : open
Orientation: palms apart
and facing each other,
RH above LH
Location: neutral space
Movement: bring palms
together

STRONG, POWER
Handshape: S : S
Orientation: bot
 palms in
Location: in front
of each shoulder
Movement: move
hands forward with a
short deliberate movement

**WEAK, FATIGUE,
FEEBLE**
Handshape: curved 5 : open
Orientation: palms facing
each other, right fingers
in left palm
Location: neutral space
Movement: collapse right fingers
into left palm with a double
movement

HIGH
Handshape: H
Orientation: palm left,
fingers pointing forward
Location: in front of right
side of chest
Movement: upward to
near right side of head

LOW, DEMOTE
Handshape: bent : bent
Orientation: hands apart,
palms facing each other
Location: in front of each
side of chest
Movement: move hands
downward

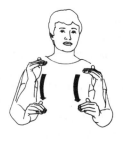

FUTURE
Handshape: open
Orientation: palm left,
fingers pointing up
Location: right cheek
Movement: forward in a
double arc while turning the
fingers forward

LATER, AFTER A WHILE, AFTERWARD
Handshape: L
Orientation: palm left, fingers pointing up
Location: right cheek
Movement: forward, ending with index finger pointing forward

TOMORROW
Handshape: 10
Orientation: palm left
Location: right cheek
Movement: forward while twisting thumb up

NEXT, NEXT TO
Handshape: open : open
Orientation: both palms facing in, fingers pointing toward each other, RH closer to chest than LH
Location: neutral space
Movement: move RH in an arc over LH, ending with right palm on back of LH

DAILY, CASUAL, DOMESTIC, EVERYDAY, ORDINARY, ROUTINE, USUAL
Handshape: A
Orientation: palm left
Location: right cheek
Movement: slide right knuckles forward with a short repeated movement

EARLY
Handshape: 5 : open
Orientation: both palms down, RH above LH
Location: neutral space
Movement: move bent middle finger of right hand forward across back of LH

STILL, YET
Handshape: Y
Orientation: palm down
Location: in front of right side of body
Movement: forward and upward in an arc
Note: This sign may be formed with two hands.

UNTIL
Handshape: 1 : 1
Orientation: RH palm
down, finger pointing left;
LH palm right, finger
pointing up
Location: neutral space
Movement: move right index
finger in an arc to touch left
index finger

OCCASIONALLY,
ONCE IN A WHILE,
PERIODICALLY,
SOMETIMES
Handshape: bent
Orientation: palm in,
fingers pointing left
Location: in front of right
side of chest
Movement: forward in a series of arcs

AGO, LAST, PAST, WAS,
WERE
Handshape: curved
Orientation: palm back,
fingers pointing up
Location: in front of right shoulder
Movement: move hand back
over shoulder, ending with
palm down and fingers pointing back

PREVIOUS
Handshape: bent
Orientation: palm down, fingers pointing back
Location: near right shoulder
Movement: tap fingertips on shoulder with a double movement

LONG TIME AGO, LONG AGO
Handshape: open
Orientation: palm left, fingers up
Location: in front of right shoulder
Movement: move hand back over shoulder, ending with fingers pointing back

BEFORE, PRE-, PRECEDING, PRIOR
Handshape: open : open
Orientation: both palms in, fingers pointing toward each other,
Location: neutral space; RH closer to chest than LH
Movement: move RH in toward chest

YESTERDAY
Handshape: Y
Orientation: palm forward
Location: right side of chin
Movement: touch thumb
to cheek near chin and
then higher on the right
cheek

RECENTLY
Handshape: X
Orientation: palm back
Location: right side of chin
Movement: bend index
finger with a double
movement

YET, NOT YET
Handshape: open
Orientation: palm back,
fingers pointing down
Location: near right side
of waist
Movement: wave fingers
back with a double movement
Note: This sign may be formed
with both hands.

**NOW, CURRENT,
PRESENT, PREVAILING,
URGENT**
Handshape: bent : bent
Orientation: both palms up
Location: in front of each
side of the body
Movement: move hands down
 with a short deliberate movement

TODAY
Handshape: bent : bent
Orientation: both palms up
and apart
Location: in front of each
side of the body
Movement: move hands
downward with a short
double movement

**AGAIN, REITERATE,
REPEAT**
Handshape: bent : open
Orientation: both palms up
Location: neutral space
Movement: bring RH up
and touch the fingers in
left palm, ending with right
palm down

TONIGHT
Compound Sign:
NOW + NIGHT

OFTEN, FREQUENTLY
Handshape: bent :
open
Orientation: both
palms up and apart
Location: neutral
space
Movement: touch
right fingertips on the left palm,
first on the fingers and then on the heel

REGULARLY, APPROPRIATE,
PROMPTLY, PROPERLY
Handshape: 1 : 1
Orientation: palms facing
in opposite directions,
index fingers angled up
Location: neutral space
Movement: brush little-
finger side of RH in a double
circular movement on index-finger side of LH

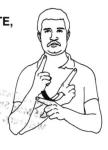

**SOMETIMES,
OCCASIONAL**
Handshape: 1 : open
Orientation: RH palm in,
finger pointing down over
left palm; LH palm up
Location: neutral space
Movement: move right index
finger in a repeated upward circular
movement, striking left palm each time

**PRESENTLY, HERE.
PRESENT**
Handshape: curved : curved
Orientation: hands apart,
palms up, fingers pointing
forward
Location: neutral space
Movement: toward each
other in flat circles

Index